AWARENESS, INSIGHT & MINDFULNESS

3 STEPS ON THE PATH TO WISDOM

AWARENESS, INSIGHT

& MINDFULNESS

3 STEPS ON THE PATH TO WISDOM

By
Randy Bell

Published by

McKee Learning Foundation

ISBN-13:   978-0-9895428-4-5

Published by:
        McKee Learning Foundation

For more information, contact:

        Info@McKeeLearningFoundation.com

        www.McKeeLearningFoundation.com

TABLE OF CONTENTS

* * * * * * * * *

To Barbara, Gay, Gwen, Joyce, Jude,
Karen, Lady, Linda, Rebecca, Sallie

whose patient listening and thoughtful discussions
served as the impetus for this book.

* * * * * * * * *

I. INTRODUCTION

We are not suddenly "enlightened"
where previously we were not.
Instead, we progressively and continually
become more enlightened.
Enlightenment is not an event. It is a process.

In many spiritual discussions occurring today, the words Awareness, Insight and Mindfulness are encountered quite frequently. We are encouraged to be more aware, achieve insight, and live mindfully "in the present moment." The goal of mindfulness, primarily achieved through personal meditation practices, has moved out of the spiritual hall, and expanded into the workplace, the schools, and the prisons.

These themes have become more prominent as an outcome of the Insight Meditation movement which began in the mid-1970s. This movement was spearheaded primarily from the considerable efforts of early practitioners like Sharon Saltzburg, Jack Kornfield, and Joseph Goldstein, co-founders of the Insight Meditation Society in central Massachusetts.

The Insight Meditation movement draws its ideas and form from the Vipassana meditation practices of the Theravada tradition of Buddhism, which is found predominately in the countries of southeast Asia. The Theravada tradition sees itself as most closely following the original teachings and practices of the historical Buddha from 2500 years ago. In these original teachings, "Insight" – seeing all things as they truly are in their complete fullness,

1

rather than as we presume them to be or desire them to be – was a primary emphasis for the Buddha. Living in "ignorance" – i.e. in our misconceptions about the reality of things – is the cause of our human suffering. Therefore it is in seeing the truest reality of things that human suffering can be ended. Ending human suffering was the primary goal of the Buddha's teachings, as explained in his Four Noble Truths along with the Noble Eightfold Path to enlightenment. Being Aware, Insightful, and Mindful are some of the critical keys to achieving the enlightenment that we seek.

Unfortunately, over time these three words have become highly overused, and many widely varying interpretations and practices of "awareness," "insight" and "mindfulness" have been established. However well intentioned, the result has been that their meanings have often become ambiguous and confusing to the spiritual seeker. The words have become overly simplified even as the ideas within them have become increasingly challenging to us. Thereby, the more precise meanings of these words, and therefore their usefulness in assisting us in our spiritual journey, have been sorely diminished. "Be here now" may make for an intriguing bumper sticker, but it says little about where "here" is or when "now" is.

We need to understand that each of these words, and the ideas behind them, are not synonymous but instead are distinct concepts. Yet they are also interrelated, linear, and mutually supportive concepts. They have great power to continually guide us in our spiritual quest. But for them to be effective, it is important to develop a clear understanding of these terms, the ideas that drive them, and the relationships among them. We need to understand that we must work not just with one or another of these concepts, but with all of them together in order to achieve the benefit of their collective power.

The Buddha's emphasis on sensitizing our awareness to all that surrounds us, achieving insight into their meanings, and drawing from those insights the ability to live a more conscious life, provides the drive for the individual seeker's quest for

2

enlightenment and the end of suffering for him-/herself. Toward that end, the individual practices, working together, of being Aware, achieving Insight, and living Mindfully are key tools to assist us spiritually. Consider the following highly simplified example:

1. You smell an apparent gas leak in your house. This is Awareness.

2. You realize that this gas has the power to explode and kill you. This is Insight.

3. You get the hell out of the house. This is Mindfulness.

In the discussions that follow, we will look at each of these concepts – Awareness, Insight, Mindfulness, "the A-I-M Triad" – in more depth. We will as well clarify how they come together as a 3-wheeled vehicle to move us on our life's spiritual journey. However, a caveat is necessary here. The intent of these discussions is to share with you some ideas on these concepts, and present a way of organizing them in your mind so as to help make them more effective tools for guiding your life's experiences. These are reflective of my own efforts at understanding and practicing these concepts. However, there are some Buddhist Insight tradition teachers who might very well and understandably argue against these interpretations and ways of structuring. I leave it to your discerning judgment as to whether these perceptions are worthy of your consideration and of benefit to you.

"People usually consider walking
on water or in thin air a miracle.
But I think the real miracle is not to walk
either on water or in thin air,
but to walk on earth.

Every day we are engaged in a miracle
which we don't even recognize:
a blue sky, white clouds, green leaves ,
the black, curious eyes of a child –
our own two eyes. All is a miracle."

— Thich Nhat Hanh, Zen Buddhist monk

II. AWARENESS

"The most basic precept of all is to be aware of
what we do, what we are, each minute.
Every other precept will follow from that."
— Thich Nhat Hanh, Zen Buddhist monk

"Awareness" is the starting point for the Awareness-Insight-Mindfulness Triad. It is the first step in subsequently moving towards Insight and then into Mindfulness.

Awareness is about "noticing." It is noticing for its own sake, without the need to form judgments or make interpretations in those moments of noticing. Awareness is about ending our usual obliviousness within which we typically pass through our day, obliviousness to our broader selves and surroundings. It is about paying attention to what is happening *around* and *within* us. It is becoming fully observant of all the many things – people, circumstances, events, environment – that encompass our life. It is about not living our life on autopilot, stuck in routine motions, schedules, and habits, acting without thinking. It is noticing in the everyday something that normally escapes our attention, "seeing something again for the first time." It is no longer wondering "where did the day go?" as we go to bed at night, because our life is now filled with the wonders of the everyday.

Awareness understands that normally we see only what we choose to see, or what others choose to reveal to us. Life happens on many levels, and does so on a very busy schedule. Much of our life is the clanging noise and clutter of surviving within the human form in a community setting of defined orders and structures. Trying to keep up with it all forces us to make choices about our time and priorities. The result is that much of the totality of our life is easily missed. Given these demands on our time and attention, we come to recognize that our vision is inherently limited unless we *proactively* work to expand it, focusing on the most important components of our life. The good news is that, with deliberate effort, we can consciously expand our skill of Awareness – that is in our power.

In Awareness, we position ourselves as an "Observer," even in situations where we may also be an active participant. As an Observer, our goal is to simply see, notice, describe, mentally document, and catalog for future investigation. We notice things previously unnoticed, receive new information of which we had not been aware, open ourselves to the idea that there is always more for us to know, in situations such as:

- An Event: something has happened that we had not noticed before.

     Things are constantly changing all around us, yet somehow many of these escape our daily attention as we blindly follow our set routines. For example, on one of our morning drives to work, we suddenly notice that a familiar house alongside our route is no longer there. Where did it go? (As it turns out, it had burned down weeks ago.) In Awareness, we are constantly looking for what has changed in the framework of our life.

- Existence: something is there (or not).

     In our daily routine, we are often oblivious to things that are in front of us each day. We go about our business of doing things, but our mind is elsewhere. So perhaps we no longer see the homeless person that continues to be in our path as we do our morning jog each day. We fail to notice that the waitress that serves us our coffee every morning no longer has her wedding band on her finger. In Awareness, we look up and see what is in front of us, and see what is to our left, right, and behind us.

- Expanded View: a new facet of something familiar is revealed.

  We often think we have the complete picture of something, know all there is to know about that something. Yet occasionally some trigger brings us a new awareness that can no longer be ignored, an Awareness that there is more underneath the surface of that something than what we have previously seen. For example, we fail to realize a long-overdue truth that our son is gay. Or that an older neighbor is a holocaust survivor, a silent witness to history. An event such as these can be a profound wake-up call, and challenge the firmness of our beliefs or our understandings of who another truly is. In Awareness, we seek to know more, and remain open to whatever that "more" may be, no matter how challenging.

- Facts: new information becomes available.

  We think of our facts as fixed givens, unchanging and immutable. Yet they are often disproven when we open ourselves to considering other points of view or information sources. Think of pre-Columbus' discovery of America, thoroughly overturning the world's longstanding belief that the world is flat, not round. It brought a rapid reworking of all the navigational maps of the Renaissance. Or more currently, for those fearful of the worldwide terrorism movement attributed to some followers of Islam, it is the realization that the warriors in ISIS who currently create much of the international terror make up only about .00001 of the world's Muslim population of three billion. In Awareness, we hold a cautious skepticism about what we believe, and continually seek out additional information that refines and balances our beliefs.

- Perspective: we begin to see things through the eyes of others as they see and experience them.

  We often act out of the belief that our view of the world, and our personal experiences and life history, are generally universal to everyone. We are therefore often confused

7

about why people act outside of our "norm," especially those people who live at a distance from us. In actuality, our perceptions of Truth and Reality are slanted by such things as the point in history in which we live, varying culture and heritage, distinct geography, our gender, our economic background and status, our education, and our own personal experiences over the course of our life. Each of these conditions creates deep inputs into our perception of what Life is and how it should be lived. Yet even under the most similar of conditions, my experiences, and hence my perceptions, are still markedly different from yours.

For example, what are the chances that a 10-year-old child living in the brutally war-torn Middle East, who has known only years of bombings and killings and hunger, will grow up seeing the world as an American 10-year-old living on a mid-western dairy farm? How different is one's daily life when one lives in an affluent suburban community versus an economically struggling inner city? How can we understand the mindset of another if we have never spoken directly to someone from those set of circumstances? In Awareness, before we make judgments of right and wrong, we accept that others have a different life experience than we, and understanding their actions or thinking requires us to better understand and appreciate a point of view drawn from a significantly different life experience than our own.

> *In Awareness, we acknowledge*
> *how little we know.*
> *By being so open, we find ourselves*
> *saying more often,*
> *"Wow, I never saw that before."*

Awareness is usually stimulated from external sources, somehow managing to break through our normally self-focused state,. Events and people find their ways to force us to notice them. The tools for receiving this Awareness come from using our five senses: hearing, tasting, seeing, smelling, and touching. In our pursuit of a greater state of Awareness, we accept that it is not all about us, that we do not occupy the space at the Center of the Universe. Rather, we proactively *seek* to notice the greater Life that is within and around us.

"Do not read so much.
Look about you and
think of what you see there."
— Richard Feynman, physicist

SOME EXAMPLES OF OUR AWARENESS:

- Awareness of the *physical sensations* within our body;
    Our body is in a constant state of change, continuously sending information to our mind as it competes to be noticed and attended to. In Awareness, we do not deny these messages. We are consistently checking in and listening to what our body is trying to tell us about our physical being. For example, we notice the places of tension in our body, the areas where pain is noticeable, thereby causing our attention to be drawn to the parts. Or conversely, we realize that our body is in a state of calm relaxation, giving us a sense of being whole. In Awareness we accept that headaches are not a call for aspirin to mask the pain, but rather are a mechanism for telling us a larger story about ourselves, a fundamental need to be addressed. As one person once observed, perhaps in a more dramatic way, "Death is nature's way of telling you to slow down."

- Awareness of the *feelings* and *emotions* we have to stimuli, people or events;

    Our emotions are powerful responses to our surroundings, and can open us to many messages about our surroundings and our selves. In Awareness, we simply give full embrace to these feelings and accept that they are present in us. However, our ability to sense that Awareness depends upon us eliminating judgments about our emotions, and instead simply recognizing them as what they are and that they are within us. Decisions about *acting* on our emotions – and whether we judge them "good" or "bad" – will be determined later in the Insight and Mindfulness stages. In Awareness, we allow ourselves to feel our pain in reacting to a child suffering in our arms, or the feelings from the loss of a loved one or the joy of accomplishing a long-term goal. We do not argue with *Why* we are experiencing these feelings, or from what deep places they come. We do not try to block out and run away from these profound feelings. We just experience them.

- Awareness of the *thoughts* in our mind;

    We are constantly bombarded with Thoughts. By some estimates, we have over 50,000 thoughts every day. They may be individual or sequences of thoughts that arise naturally in our mind – either deliberately or seemingly on their own – many of which we often rush to censor according to what is "proper" or what fits our self-image. In Awareness, we acknowledge that these thoughts exist, but in and of themselves they are just that – Thoughts, with no inherent substance. They are simply constructs of our own making from our creative imagination. Instead of censoring the "bad" thoughts, or self-congratulating ourselves on the "good" thoughts, we avoid any labels whatsoever. We simply reserve our thoughts for later exploration as to what stands behind them, and what larger messages to us that they may contain. In Awareness, we let the surprising nasty thought we have about someone arise

10

in our mind, even as we leave it unspoken. As well, a shocking thought of doing violence to ourselves or others. None of these thoughts are actions, they are just thoughts. They are there fighting for attention whether we want to acknowledge them or not. Allowing our Awareness of them to enter our consciousness allows us to then deal with them subsequently as they need to be dealt with. And then discarded.

- Observing the *environment* around you;

    In Awareness, we make a point of noticing the buildings, wildlife, vegetation, scenery, and people on the street as we pass by them. Further, we take time and make effort to note some detailed or distinctive characteristics about them beyond just their surface presentation. We inherently know that each of these objects can subsequently provide a wealth of source material for our learning and understanding about Life. In Awareness, we recall the expression made popular in the 1970s – "stop and smell the roses." We reinforce our awareness about how big Life truly is, how much there is for us to partake, how miraculous Creation is in its scope and its profound detail. All of which helps to re-center our place in this existence.

- Recognizing <u>in depth</u> what people are truly saying ("Deep Listening").

    Much time is spent exchanging many words on a superficial level between people who are often not paying much real attention to what is being said, or hearing the disguised implications of the words being spoken, or recognizing the emotional content behind what people are saying. It leaves one to often wonder, "did you realize what that person was *really* saying to you?" It is the shallow small talk of the cocktail party, the insincere brushoff of "let's do lunch," the cultural "southern charm" of polite vagueness juxtaposed against the bluntness of "northern directness." In Awareness, we remember that it is not just

11

about the words, it is all about the intended meaning. The emotions behind the words, the speaker's desire to be heard, the reveal of the body language, the unspoken messages. We do not just listen to every word, we also watch, ask questions, and seek to truly *understand* what is being said – by mouth, body, and expression – to us and/or to others.

Two key cautions to remember:

- **Awareness is fully welcoming, without judgments**.
  Negative judgments at the Awareness stage preclude subsequently achieving Insight or Mindfulness.

- **We do not draw any conclusions at this time**.
  Awareness is simply input. The meanings will be determined later.

In Awareness, we are slow to judgment, labels and conclusions, rather than our usual rush to hurriedly define things. Judgments, labels and conclusions are like dams shutting off the flow of Pure Awareness. Instead, we just pause and take it in. *In Pure Awareness, we have no opinions*. As soon as we begin to make decisions, Awareness stops; we cannot do both at the same time. The longer we stay in Pure Awareness, more Awareness will continue to arise.

Why do we pursue Awareness? Because it opens the door to Insight. In fact, it is the prerequisite for gaining Insight. Increasing our Awareness of small daily details leads us to Awareness of ever bigger and deeper things – and ultimately to Awareness of the Divine, the Universe, our Enlightenment, whichever we are seeking.

> *Awareness is about reawakening our <u>vision</u>,*
> *being engaged, and paying attention.*
>
> *It is being in the mind of a child,*
> *where everything is a brand new exploration.*

"I've worked all my life on the subject of awareness,
whether it's awareness of the body,
awareness of the mind,
awareness of your emotions,
awareness of your relationships,
or awareness of your environment.
I think the key to transforming your life is
to be aware of who you are."
— Deepak Chopra, spiritual teacher

III. AWARENESS:

PRACTICE EXERCISES

Do not "think" about being Aware.
Do not "search" for Awareness.
Just create space and open yourselves to it.
Let it simply arise within you.

Awareness is a skill. Like any other skill, we need to know the basic concepts of the skill. Then we have to engage in certain activities to translate those concepts into actions. For it is in action that our skills become truly meaningful and effective. Once achieved, our practice in Awareness must be continual, for our skills can easily be lost. Growing spiritually requires our constant vigilance and dedicated diligence.

The ways in which we can practice Awareness must be individualized to each person. Each of us lives in different circumstances, comes from different backgrounds, learns most effectively in different manners. So the first step in enhancing skills in Awareness is to find the methods and situations that work best for you. The following suggestions are examples of things we can do to intentionally strengthen our Awareness of ourselves and our surroundings. But they are best utilized as ideas for creating those techniques appropriate for you.

1. Take a break in the middle of some daily activity that usually consumes your concentrated attention. Take a short walk; look

14

around. Become aware of something that has been in front of you all along that you have not noticed before within these times or places.

2. Sit quietly and inconspicuously beside two people having a conversation. Analyze and make mental notes of what you hear and observe:

    - Who is actually truly engaged in this conversation?

    - Who is just passing time and being polite?

    - Who is truly listening to the other, versus just waiting for their turn to speak?

    - Who is asking clarifying questions, or inquiring for more information, regarding what a speaker is saying?

    - Who is continually trying to redirect the conversation away from the person currently speaking and turn it back to them in order to recite their experiences?

    - How is each reacting to what is being said?

    - What is *really* being said underneath or beyond the actual words?

    - What is each person feeling within this conversation?

    - What is each person trying to achieve out of this conversation and momentary relationship?

3. Pretend you are at your annual physical, and you are your own doctor. What do you write down on your chart about your current physical state of being?

> *Awareness looks deeply to see*
> *the details underneath the surface*
> *that usually escape our notice.*

4. Look very closely at a plant. Write down <u>10</u> bullet observations about what you see.

5. Sit quietly for 20 minutes. Let your mind just wander, not focusing on any one particular thing. Notice carefully the thoughts that arise; reject none, accept all. Do not try to solve anything or conclude anything. Just learn what is occurring beneath the surface of your mind, fighting for your attention.

6. Think about a tree you have seen in the past. Consider what it is, where it comes from, what makes it up, what it does. Write down <u>20</u> bullet observations about the characteristics of that tree that you remember. Then go look at that tree again in person. How does the real tree (versus your memory of it) compare to what you wrote down? What else can you say about this tree?

7. Think of a person you know. Write down at least <u>20</u> bullet observations about aspects of that person (physical; mental; characteristics; qualities) of which you are aware.

<u>An Example of an Awareness Observation</u>:
I was sitting in a workplace cafeteria one day many years ago. Looking around at the people eating there, I made a particular observation. We are told that women seek to bond with each other, particularly in times of conversation. Yet they make a great effort to dress uniquely from each other. Conversely, men are said to seek to be individualists. Yet they dress essentially the same, with only minimal variation ("the uniform").

"Why is that?" leads us into the Insight phase.

> *Awareness is a Decision*
> *you make for your Self.*

"The great awareness comes slowly, piece by piece.
The path of spiritual growth is a path of lifelong learning.
The experience of spiritual power is basically a joyful one."
— M. Scott Peck, psychiatrist

IV. OPENING TO INSIGHT

"A moment's insight is sometimes
worth a life's experience."
— Oliver Wendell Holmes, Sr., author

As we will see later in Chapter VI, Insight is about learning. Not just about learning something new, but learning something that will *change* how we see things. Change how we may have always thought about some idea or belief. Change how we have previously understood principles of Life and Creation. Change who we have believed our Self to be. Insight is about gaining knowledge that will subsequently come alive into action.

However, there are certain personal attitudes that we need to develop to be receptive to gaining such Insight. These should be continually cultivated in our meditation practice, as well as in our everyday daily activities in ways individually appropriate for us. Unless we take the initiative to first open our minds to new things, it will be impossible for the power of Insight to enter our lives.

8 Attitudes for Opening to Insight

1. *Observant:* We cultivate sensitizing our mind, eyes, and ears more deeply to things that transpire around us. Being observant helps us to strengthen our skills of Awareness. We notice, and pay attention to, the people, events, words and ideas that we normally blindly ignore as we pass through the day in rote fulfillment of our daily tasks. We look more deeply into what lies beneath the surface façade of events, people, and all things in nature. As we continually move forward, we also look

18

around for Life's wider guidance, recognizing the broader field upon which we play.

2. *Curiosity:* We cultivate a strong sense of curiosity about our Self, about Life in general, about what truly goes into making Life unfold, beyond what we simply see on the surface. If we lack a broad curiosity, we have no motivation for new understandings beyond what we already believe. Insight cannot come to an uncurious mind that is closed to new ideas, a mind that believes it already knows what is needed to be known.

3. *Compassion:* We cultivate a recognition that each person has a personal and very private story. A story that happens below the surface that we see, and beyond what we may think we know. A story that that person may barely know for him-/herself. A journey into anyone's inner being, including our own, is fraught with difficulty and misunderstanding, a maze of many false trails and dead-end arrivals. Knowing that such an inner story exists, we explore cautiously, and are slow to draw conclusions. We remind ourselves that all of us are working through our own struggles and imperfect resolutions. The company of a gentle companion, who appreciates and can sympathize with that struggle, is helpful to that difficult journey. A companion to our Self, a companion for others.

4. *Culpability:* We cultivate accepting responsibility for our own contributions to difficult situations and interactions with difficult people. When we feel mistreated or misunderstood, we are typically quick to believe all of it was the other person's fault. But we are never without some portion of culpability for what transpired. In some form and to some greater or lesser degree, we share culpability for the cause of our interaction problems, the timing of it, how the interaction was (mis-)handled or escalated, the resulting fallout, or the inability to reconcile afterwards. Even if our respective culpabilities were not "equal," finding that piece of our culpable thoughts and actions, however small, and taking personal responsibility for

them, can open widely a large door of opportunities for Insight into our Self. It is not about blaming yourself. It is about growing yourself.

5. _Non-judgment_: We cultivate more tolerance regarding the concepts of "right and wrong" and "good and bad." Instead, we begin to see ideas and actions not as having *absolute* values, but as being *relative* to particular circumstances. This is particularly true when we make judgments about the thoughts that arise within us. Thoughts are simply statements we make in our mind, whatever may be their provocation. Thoughts have no substance unless we *act* upon them – which we do only infrequently.

   When we label our thoughts as "good" or "bad," we typically also erroneously label ourselves as "good" or "bad." Similarly, when we judge the words or actions of others as either "good" or "bad," we erroneously label them a "good" or "bad" person. This easily-convenient (and premature) judgment causes us to fail to see the whole person involved. We fail to seek out and know their personal story and their motivations, and thereby, to understand what brought their words and actions to this result. We may still disagree with the choices that they made. But by avoiding unhelpful judgments, we learn something worthwhile – about our own Self as well as them – from the experience instead of just walking away from it. As the Dali Lama says, "Resist the action; love the person."

   Nothing blocks the arrival of Insight quite as much as negative judgment. Avoiding the tendency to judge our thoughts about ourselves or others allows us to safely explore the reasons for our discomforting thoughts, leading to even more Insight. It takes great courage to look inside of our Self to see precisely what is there. Non-judgment fortifies us for that inner journey.

6. _No-label_: We cultivate resisting, and seeing beyond, all the "labels" that we apply to things. We are prone to giving each

20

thing we encounter some "name" in an attempt to more easily define them into our understanding. Seeking to ostensibly gain more Insight, we counterproductively keep adding on even more burdensome labels of our own making (e.g. she is female; a parent; an employee; a doctor; a lover). We continue to do so until the original thing itself becomes nearly unrecognizable, barely able to stand up under the weight of all of these burdensome definitions and expectations. Thereby, we narrow our view of, and fail to see, the greater full potential that lives in every existing thing. Each label we apply causes us to make quick assumptions about what that label means, thereby creating expectations within us for what that something "should be" – expectations that may or may not be correct. Insight helps to take us beyond those labels, to see the true essence of the thing, to see its greater scope and potential, shorn of the burden of our own definitions that we place upon them.

7. *Openness:* We cultivate the ability to easily *consider* new thoughts and ideas that are different than what we currently have. We may ultimately determine that those new thoughts and ideas are not appropriate for us. But we arrive at that conclusion only after honest investigation and open deliberation, not just because they are different than what we have been taught or come to believe. We seek to be a "clean slate," not rejecting things out of hand. We let our Insight, not our past, lead us to our conclusions. We welcome periodic opportunities to revisit our ideas to see if they are still worthwhile. We do not define Who we are by What we believe, because we understand that we are a constantly changing, growing human being. We continually ask our Self, are we prepared to throw out something we currently believe if we discover a greater Truth?

8. *Commitment:* We cultivate a commitment to returning to the practice of Insight over and over again. We understand that Insight is a temporary place, a state of understanding that we

will enjoy upon arrival, but from which we must subsequently leave in order to move to even more new places. There is always more for us to learn, even about the same topic, such as additional nuances, adjustments for circumstances, different possible ways to view the same thing. And so we remain in continuing motion in our journey toward Insight.

Why are these Eight Attitudes important? Because Insight is intrinsically about *Change*. Change within Us. Seeing things differently than before. Changing what we believe is always hard, and is not our natural choice; it always feels easier to stay within what we already know. But that does not make for a life lived fully. Without cultivating these Eight Attitudes, without the willingness to change our perspectives and beliefs where warranted, Insight *will not happen* regardless of the amount of time spent in thought or reflection. The good news is that these Eight Attitudes can be practiced and applied to our thinking and actions throughout the day, as well as during our reflective meditation times. With practice, Insight, and then Change, come more easily.

There are a number of practices one can utilize to bring greater Insight into one's consciousness. Practices of quiet time alone, structured meditation, personal reflection, or spiritual contemplation. But whatever practices one may choose to utilize, cultivating these 8 Attitudes for Opening to Insight in our daily living and in our spiritual practice is a necessary prerequisite. Insight is not something we chase, an inspiration we imagine, or a conclusion we create by thinking. We do not pursue Insight by wandering about aimlessly and knocking on myriad closed doors that surround us. Instead, we discover it by opening the door into our inner being, where Insight already lives waiting for our invitation to arise, and letting it enter into our consciousness.

"... [Insight] comes when we are not necessarily looking for it, or straining to make it happen. [So] we must ... live in a posture of readiness for whenever insight might surprise us. When insight comes, we must be willing to wrestle with the changes of perspective that it potentially demands of us and desires to bring to our lives. We must be willing to set aside our presumptions of how things 'should be' and open our deepest selves to the possibilities of life ..."
— Tyana Yonkers, Professor of Religion

V. OPENING TO INSIGHT:

PRACTICE EXERCISES

*Perform Your Own Self-Assessment
Of Your Openness.*

1. Currently, each of us is likely to be stronger or more comfortable with certain of the Attitudes than others. Examine each of the *8 Attitudes of Opening to Insight* as they pertain to you. For each Attitude, write down your assessment regarding the extent to which you are open to that pathway as a way for Insight to enter your consciousness:

   - Which one(s) feels strong and natural for me?

   - Which one(s) feels weak or unnatural for me?

   - Why are the weak one(s) hard or unnatural for me?

   - Which one(s) would I like to focus on strengthening for now?
       (Don't try to take on too many efforts at once.)

   - What Practice Steps can I take to strengthen my "weak" Attitude(s)?

2. As often as possible, set aside time at the end of the day and review the list of 8 Attitudes.

- With each one, write down any instances in the day in which you *proactively* and *intentionally* evidenced that Attitude.

- In those instances, is there something you might have done differently?

- Were there any situations where you let an opportunity for Opening go by – either intentionally, or because you just did not see it at the time?

- Based upon your daily review, what will be your Intention, or the Practice Steps you will take, regarding an "Opening" Attitude that you will seek to emphasize tomorrow?

SUGGESTION: "Opening to Insight" is a repetitive, practiced skill. If your time at end of the day for assessing your efforts is limited, you might try focusing on just one Attitude on a given day, shifting your emphasis throughout the course of the week.

> ". . . I feel we don't really need scriptures.
> The entire life is an open book, a scripture. Read it.
> Learn while digging a pit or
> chopping some wood or cooking some food.
> If you can't learn from your daily activities,
> how are you going to understand the scriptures?"
> — Swami Satchidananda, yoga teacher

VI. INSIGHT INTO INSIGHT

"The most fundamental aggression to ourselves,
the most fundamental harm we can do to ourselves,
is to remain ignorant by not having
the courage and the respect
to look at ourselves honestly and gently."
— Pema Chödrön, Tibetan Buddhist nun

The pursuit of Insight is a primary focus for all Buddhist traditions, even as the approach may vary among these traditions. Yet Insight is a pursuit appropriate for all people, whether Buddhist or any other religious affiliation, or even in a secular context. Insight is that which helps us grow into maturity intellectually, emotionally and spiritually. Nevertheless, gaining Insight requires great effort and diligence on our part.

Insight is seeing the bigger picture in all things and all experiences, engaging our "big mind" (universal mind) of broad understanding versus our usual "small mind" (relative mind) that sees things merely on their day-to-day surface. Insight is the ability to see the seemingly random events that occur in our life as in fact links in a connecting chain of our life experiences. It is about seeing the larger patterns that encompass our seemingly everyday occurrences. It is what Lama Surya Das calls that "aha" moment when we encounter a sudden and fresh understanding of that which we thought we already knew – about people, things, ideas, experiences, and Life – only to realize that, in fact, we knew only a small piece of that picture.

Insight is discovering the True Reality of things at their core essence, whether a person, other life form, relationship, event, place, culture, idea, opinion, belief, or fact. We strip away our personal attachments, labels, adornments, illusions, prior teachings, and beliefs to see what then remains. With Insight, we see things not as we may have wanted them to be, or thought them to be, but as they truly are. Insight is a progressive unveiling over time, a never-ending learning, as we gradually *become* enlightened. Once we gain Insight, we accept the essential nature of that True Reality, giving up any clinging desire that it would change, or be something other than what it is. Rather, we willingly accept the challenge that what we can change is Us, and the manner in which we choose to react and respond to that True Reality.

Insight comes to us in a variety of moments and ways. We start with Awareness, the trigger, the noticing of what we have not seen before. We pass through our various Attitudes for Opening to Insight, continually creating a receptivity for Insight within ourselves. We arrive at the moment of Insight: the "Therefore"; the "*Now* I understand." If Awareness is Input, Insight is Conclusion. If Awareness is Noticing; Insight is Understanding.

In our pursuit of a more conscious and enlightened state, we can achieve Insight into our Self. We can achieve Insight into others. We can achieve Insight into our surroundings   , and Insight into Life – its component parts and how they all work together. We can achieve Insight into how things and relationships interact. We can achieve Insight into the larger meanings of everyday events. And we can achieve Insight into the fundamental laws – physical and non-physical – of Creation itself.

> "One does not become enlightened
> by imagining figures of light,
> but by making the darkness conscious.
> The latter procedure, however, is disagreeable
> and therefore not popular."
> — C.G. Jung, psychoanalyst

10 Themes of Insight

Insight can occur within many different themes of realization. Within each of these general themes, there are many detailed individual realizations that can surface. The following are some categories illustrating the broad territory over which our Insight can roam. (Note that there is certainly some overlap among these various themes.)

1. An <u>expanded understanding</u> that sees an Object's full potential.

   As a human being, each of us is a mix of skills, talents, personalities. Not all of these traits have been realized or are expressed equally. Some stand out as dominant, such that they likely define us to others (and to ourselves). Others recede into the background but exist nonetheless, perhaps waiting for their appropriate time to surface. Each one of us wears many "hats" and labels as we go through life. Some are there only for a short period; others stay with us throughout our existence. Every Object, both human and nonhuman, goes through stages of change, taking on many forms over time, even though we may often wish otherwise. A stone is not cast in stone.

   From Awareness, we become sensitive to the existence of these many parts and facets in all things. In Insight, we seek to see all that makes up an Object of our attention, and the full potential of what it is and can be. We condition our acceptance of the usual attached labels, recognizing that they are just temporary parts of a much larger whole. We need to see the parts; we are obligated discover the whole.

2. A <u>changed opinion</u> that alters a presumed belief.

   At any given moment, we are an inexhaustible collection of opinions, beliefs and perspectives. We typically hold on tightly to that list, because we believe that list is not just what we believe, but it actually defines who we are as a person, who "I" am. Yet over the course of our life new information is constantly presenting itself to us, information that may well contradict our previously-held beliefs. Our religious training may have given us one understanding of how the earth and all that inhabit it were created. Yet science offers us a number of other scenarios, or at least more explicit details as to how these events may have been effected. We may have learned a particular view of God and the Universe, only to find conflicts with that view as we go through our everyday living, causing us to question whether God is not who we thought him/her/it to be. Two centuries ago, owning human slaves was seen as a measure of wealth and sign of economic success. Today we disallow such ownership as an abhorrent relationship between one human being and another. As a young person entering adulthood, we often believe we know all we need to know. But as the old anecdote observes, "I was amazed how much my parents had learned between when I started and when I finished college!"

From Awareness, we become sensitive to new information presenting itself in our every moment from every corner of our Life. In Insight, we do not jump willy-nilly from one opinion to the next with little concern or thoughtfulness. Rather, our goal is to form our beliefs and understandings from deep thinking and careful consideration. But we always know that our beliefs are incomplete, that they reflect available knowledge known to us only to that moment. There is always more to learn. So when new information presents itself to us, whether by the process of Insight or other means, we greet this fresh information as a new friend, here to open new doors of growth for us. Our old belief was not "wrong"; our new belief is not "better." We have simply achieved yet another milestone, arrived at a new place, from which to continue on with our journey.

3. A <u>recurring pattern</u> overlays an individual event.

We tend to see our life as a series of individual events, disconnected from each other, happening independently at random. But when we stop to examine these events carefully, and line them up alongside of each other, we likely see a very definite recurring pattern of actions. Places may change; different people may be present; times and circumstances change; new words and descriptions may be said. Yet when we strip away these surface appearances, and look structurally at these life events, we see that, in fact, they are all the same. Our life's events have some pattern(s) in common that lead us into and out of these situations. Our script is a recurring story.

Perhaps we have a pattern of reacting very badly when we encounter a particular triggering situation, regardless of whom or what is involved. Perhaps we get a nagging sense of anxiousness when our life begins to fall into too set a routine. One of the best examples of a recurring pattern involves a history of repeatedly changing jobs after only a relatively short period of employment. The boss mistreats us; our coworkers do not respect us; the work is boring; there are too many stressful expectations put upon us, etc. All seemingly valid arguments for leaving when taken at face value. Except that our recurring pattern is that no job is ever good enough; there are always too many demands; we always leave without a resolution; we start the cycle all over again. The common denominator in all of this is – US. Not the bosses, not the work, not the environment. Us. Our friends, who likely supported us in our early job dissatisfactions, now have heard it all too many times before – the initial excitement of the "new perfect job"; the inevitable crestfallen crash to earth a year or two later over the "job from hell."

From Awareness, we become sensitive to the subtle sense of having "been here before." In Insight, we begin to see what our friends see. We begin to see the patterns that we follow over and over again. These are not new, random events being inflicted upon us. Instead, they reflect a consistent pattern we have set and now follow in the conduct of our lives. We may have seen our life as a line-item list of disconnected events; in Insight, we now see that we have been caught up in a vicious cycle of our own making that we need to get out from under. It is a picture difficult for us to see through the foggy glasses of our introspection. But see it we can. See it we must if we are to live a free, enlightened life.

4. Larger conclusions can be drawn from simple observations.
    When we encounter something, we typically see that object – a person, a thing, an idea, a piece of nature – as something unto itself. Self-contained. But if we take time to think about it more deeply, we can see beyond that surface into a much larger theme, a clue to solving a greater mystery. It is said that a sculptor looks at a large slab of rock, and sees within it something we cannot see – a work of art inside waiting to be released by that sculptor's trained and creative hands. A forester looks at a tree, and sees all of its many component parts – roots, trunk, bark, limbs, leaves, blossoms – all combining and working together. Over the course of one year of that tree's life, contained therein is a representation of the life-cycle of all creation. Looking at the birds who visit and nest in that tree, the ornithologist understands that a bird never bothers to ask itself, "What is my Life Purpose?" Instead, it follows its intuition and simply goes about its work to realize that Purpose. The builder looks at the large, protective wall she has just built – whether physical or mental – and thinks,

31

"The walls we build to protect us are the same walls that imprison us inside."

From Awareness, we become sensitive to stopping and observing things more closely. In Insight, we recognize that all objects – all people, beings, things, events, conversations – inherently contain subtle but pertinent messages for us. Messages we receive only when we open ourselves to receiving them. Messages we hear only when we are truly listening, see only when we are truly looking, understand only when we are thinking clearly and broadly. Insight occurs when we make time to be reflective and insightful, and allow our unyielding curiosity to run freely.

5. <u>Things are fundamentally the same</u> when stripped of their surface adornments.

At a surface level, we are each a unique person. Each snowflake, each pebble on the seashore, each leaf on the tree is said to be unique. Yet science tells us that all objects at their core – human, plant, animal, matter – are built from the same working material. For all our human distinctiveness, each of our human forms is constructed from common building blocks of cells, DNA, microscopic particles beyond the reach of the human eye. In our molecular makeup, there is more "blank space" than there is "filled space," yet we seem pretty solid, and see no gaps, when we look at each other.

From Awareness, we become sensitive to seeing commonalities that exist across Objects. In Insight, we realize that we all come from the same "stuff," yet that stuff has been assembled in unique combinations to create the individual Self that we are so fond of presenting to the world. It is yet another of Life's many paradoxes: we are all the same; we are all different. We understand that all parents within any cultural community seek to love and protect their children; there are some universal traits that transcend artificial bounds. While we may be enamored of some famous individual, or our boss, or our parent, Insight tells us that each of them is "just a person." A person worthy of our respect and admiration, perhaps, but also still just a person made from and driven by the same makeup as you and me. In Insight, we live comfortably in the bilateral world of uniqueness and commonality, recognize both within all things, and see the unity that results from that bilateral world.

6. <u>Underlying causes</u> lie beneath surface actions.

Things do not actually happen "out of the blue." Every action has a cause. Every action is preceded by a thought, a thought that itself comes from a series of predecessor thoughts built upon our life story of past experiences. The door to exploring this journey of thoughts opens for us when we find ourselves confused when we examine our reactions to a given incident that occurs. A reaction that we sense is out of proportion to the occurrence itself. Something happens in our daily interactions, and we react strongly, excessively, to it. Even though we tell ourselves that is was a valid reaction on our part to the triggering event, something inside of us wonders, "Where did *that* reaction come from? Why did I get so angry over such a simple thing? Why was I so smitten with that [person / moment]?" Someone cuts in line in front of us, and we angrily question, "Why do they get to do what I cannot do by virtue of the moral code I was taught?" An offer for a new job, or a promotion, or a new lifestyle comes our way, and we wonder, "Why was I so resistant to accepting that new opportunity?

From Awareness, we become sensitive to observing our reactions and their appropriateness to the situations we find ourselves in. In Insight, we look to uncover those hidden causes, which will then allow us to understand our true and undisguised Self. Retracing backwards through that maze of neural pathways in in our mind is the most thrilling, frightening, enlightening, and astounding adventure that we will take in our lifetime. We use our anger as a tool for Insight, accepting the Truth that anger directed outward toward others actually reflects anger directed inward to our self. Answering the question of why we are angry requires a step-by-step search, from one answer to the next, peeling away clues one at a time, until we find ourselves back at a fundamental core place of knowing. "So *that* is what was actually going on in the moment. That is what I was truly thinking!" After the dust of the upsetting moment settles, a fantastic voyage to Insight within the mind awaits us.

7. Things happen for a reason.

As we said above regarding the topic of causation, things do not actually happen "out of the blue." While our life may often seem to a series of herky-jerky erratic lurches from one thing to the next, there is likely a unifying thread that runs through this unfolding story. Our life is a book, not a paragraph. It is a book filled with many chapters, a main character, many supporting players coming in and going out, a story line that chronicles a narrative through endless scenes, plot twists, and adventure tales. It is a seemingly unending story, always awaiting the next turning of the page. It is a *continuing* story, always on the move, always unfolding, rarely as dull as we might think it to be.

From Awareness, we become sensitive to a feeling of connection in the phases, and to the parts, that make up our Life. In Insight, we accept that this connected thread exists within our life story. And so we seek to read our own story in order to understand how that thread has unfolded. Not just for amusement (although we may find very amusing chapters within our story), but to appreciate what and who has gone into making our life what it has been – and is still becoming. We appreciate the roles people have played in or life, roles perhaps very different than what we may have believed at the time. Rather than just individual events, we see the linkages in our life, that our life has unfolded by moving from one stepping stone to the next on our unique personal path. We see that over time, in one form or fashion, we have drawn from, modified and reused everything we have previously done and learned. Our life is our karma. And yes, karma is a bitch. With this greater Insight, we now have the opportunity to truly choose what our next stepping stones will be, and how we will step to them.

8. An <u>exaggerated sense of Self</u> prevents us from seeing more objective Truths.

> I am the center of the known and unknown Universe. I am the locus and focal point for all that happens. It is all about me. Even if things are happening in a distant place, it is not until I read about it, and determine if/how it affects me, that it becomes truly real. And whatever does in fact happen to me, it is personal, because it is all about me. In my own mind, I am very clear about this. Even though you also think you are the genuine center, I know better, even if I do not say so. I smile, knowing that you will come to this same realization soon enough. The realization that it is all about me.

> In quieter, unthreatened times, our logical mind gets hold of this thought perspective and calls us to task. We restore a sense of balance and humility to our thinking. We

understand that self-centered ego blinds us to other perspectives, perspectives as valid as our own. Other perspectives that may be different, but have an element of truth within them that rounds out and completes our knowledge. Self-centered ego blinds us to other people's circumstances, and prevents us from appreciating, and empathizing with, the plights of other.

From Awareness, we become sensitive to all the time and words we spend focused on "I." In Insight, we come to understand that we are not the center of the Universe, but only the center of our own experiences. And even that center is limited, because it does not allow for the recognition of how many other influences are embedded within the experiences we have. "Why is this happening to *me*?" is not just over-personalization, it also defeats our sense of humility – that most precious characteristic of a spiritual person – that seeks to remind us that we are a part of a much larger Universal story. Insight reminds us that our rained-out picnic is a life-saving rain for the struggling farmer fighting off drought. Insight keeps us continually seeing that bigger picture, our eyes wide open.

9. <u>All things are connected</u>.
    We do not live in an isolated vacuum, separated from our surroundings. In some aspects of our human life, we are on our own for most of the end results. But even that "on our own" nature is limited. For there is little or nothing we can do that can be done without the involvement of other resources. Even that most fundamental facet of life – breathing – requires the work of countless other forces (human and nature) to generate the oxygen needed and bring it to us. We think most often in terms of our separateness, which is why most religions expend such efforts to bring us back to our connectedness. The

Buddhists talk about "no-self," meaning that there is nothing that exists independently, solely on its own inherent is-ness. An old African pays homage by saying that, "I am because my ancestors were." At Zen mealtimes, the group may chant, "72 labors brought us this food; we should know how it comes to us." The Christian teachings continually call upon us to "love thy neighbor as thyself." Islam exhorts Muslims to be gracious hosts in their homes to strangers and guests – we are all neighbors.

From Awareness, we become sensitive to our feelings of connection, and discomfort with disconnection, with all of surrounding Creation. In Insight, we see and accept this interconnection. We understand that the events and outcomes of our lives are interdependent with others. We spend time in reflection considering how many people we have met and spoken to in our lives – all of the people with whom we have shared our journey. How far removed have we become from those who make our lives possible? We grapple with what it would be like to be truly singular and "alone" in this world. For most of us, it is a state we would not seek, even for those who enjoy a certain degree of solitude. Insight defeats a sense of separation, and keeps us connected to the larger humanity of which we are a most integral part.

10. The Universe / Creation includes all things.

> If we so choose, Insight takes us into a deeper world of spiritual realization. It opens doors to what some consider a spiritual union with the Divine, what other might consider an exalted state of wisdom and enlightenment. In this level of Insight, we see all that there is to see. We see as Creation sees, think as Creation thinks, act as Creation would act, even within our own more limited human state of existence. In this Insight, we include all things – physical and non-

physical – as part of Creation itself, without conflict among each other. The laws of science need not conflict with our religious stories; science simply explains the tools and methods used in performing Creation. We accept all that is, each of equal importance and value in its contribution to what makes up the Universe.

From Awareness, we become sensitive to a nagging certainty that there is a greater reality that transcends what we can immediately see and touch. In Insight, we see the vast-ness of the "all" vis-à-vis the simple-ness of "me," and are not threatened by the magnitude of difference. We find resolution to our personal fears that all beings born will die or be transformed, including us, because we find acceptance that nothing is permanent, and all things change. The plaintive question of "Why did the Universe set up this aspect of Life this way?" becomes our trail guide leading us to understanding, rather than the desperate call of the aggrieved and defeated. This is Insight that leads to the greatest understandings, and those understandings give us direction, comfort, and peace.

> *IN INSIGHT, THE WORLD IS*
> *NO LONGER AS I HAD*
> *SEEN OR UNDERSTOOD*
> *IT TO BE.*
>
> *That difference changes my vision*
> *and understanding of the world,*
> *and thereby changes me.*

"Meditation is to get insight,
to get understanding and compassion,
and when you have them,
you are compelled to act."
— Thich Nhat Hanh, Zen Buddhist monk

VII. INSIGHT INTO INSIGHT:

PRACTICE EXERCISES

"When you open your mind,
you open new doors to
new possibilities for yourself
and new opportunities to help others."
— Roy T. Bennett, inspirational author

1. Think about how specific ideas and perspectives have changed for you over time. What did you once believe that now has changed? What caused that change to occur? (You may have to start with some current beliefs and work backwards in time to be aware of those that have changed.)

2. Remember back to some past instance where you had some kind of Insight occur to you.

   • What was that Insight?

   • How did it come about?

   • How did you follow up on that Insight, if at all?

   • How could you set some similar circumstances to encourage new Insights to occur?
       (Model you own best situations and environment for Insight)

3. Think about a variety of different "Objects" (a single event, person, thing, idea, etc.) you might select for pursuing Insight. Which Insight "themes" might be applicable as a framework within which to view your selected Object?

4. <u>Detailed Practice</u>: Pick a particular Object in which you would like to gain new Insight.

    • Write down what you already know (Awareness) about that Object thus far (Chapter II).

    • What "Opening to Insight" Attitudes come into play with examining this Object further (Chapter IV)?

    • What Insight Themes come into play with examining this Object further (Chapter VI)?

    • What setting and method(s) will you use to allow insight to enter your thoughts?

    • Try that approach.

    • Assess how effective your approach was in this instance. (what worked; what did not? What Insights arose; what frustrations occurred?)

> "A mind set in its ways is wasted.
> Don't do it."
> — Eric Schmidt, Chairman of Alphabet, Inc.

VIII. A MEDITATION PROCESS FOR INSIGHT

"When you have a dream, it doesn't often come at you screaming in your face: 'This is who you are. This is what you must be for the rest of your life.' Sometimes a dream almost whispers. And I've always said to my kids, the hardest thing to listen to, your instincts, your human and personal intuition, always whispers, It never shouts. Very hard to hear. So you have to, every day of your lives, be ready to hear what whispers in your ear. And if you can listen to the whisper, and if it tickles your heart, and it is something you think you want to do for the rest of your life, then that is going to be what you do for the rest of your life. And we will benefit from everything you do."

— Steven Spielberg, director

True Insight is rarely the result of logical thinking or deductive reasoning. Rather, it is an *intuitive* process that speaks to us from within. It is a process that transcends our normal processes of thinking and seeing. It is typically a *leap* in our understanding rather than our usual incremental, step-by-step process of thinking.

Insight is *not* "Thinking." Thinking is what we normally do when trying to solve a problem, learn more about something, or try to make a decision. This is what we have been taught to do from a very early stage. Thinking is the function of the ego self. When we engage in thinking, we write our own narrative stories, consciously or unconsciously leading that story into what we want it to be. We construct a seemingly intellectually logical and sequential path, starting from our Question and leading to our Answer. But in that process, we are unknowingly blinded to the flaws in our logic path, our lack of complete information, our own predispositions, even as we convince ourselves that we have arrived at our conclusion "objectively." More often than not, we unintendedly jump to a conclusion we had already made, and retrofit a path to justify our pre-drawn conclusion, all done unconsciously.

Insight, however, is NOT "thinking" about something. Thinking and logical reasoning are beneficial, but they are limited by our pre-conditions – pre-conditions of what we already believe or have experienced. True Insight comes from surrendering the control our ego has over our mind and thoughts, tossing out all that we may have believed before, and performing the difficult task of "just listening" to the words of our intuitive Self.

Insight can actually happen at any time in various circumstances *if we are paying attention* and are open to receiving it. It can happen as a random thought as we are enjoying an undistracted walk enveloped by the nurturing warmth of the sights and sounds of Nature. Or during time spent in a quiet moment alone in a favorite place. Perhaps someone says something to us unexpectedly "out of the blue" that grabs our attention, and makes us want to explore that comment further. Or an unexpected event occurs in a manner that makes us wonder, "what is this about?" Occasionally, we may simply experience "a sudden burst of realization" about something, with no obvious trigger for the experience, but with an all-to-real result.

Each of these situations may provide us with a supportive environment for gaining Insight into some object of our curiosity. But they are each *reactive* vehicles, outside of our initiation. Instead, one alternative way we can approach Insight is from a *proactive* basis through the use of a structured meditation approach, using a specific form and method to pursue our intention. In such a structured method, there are two key elements that we utilize:

- Determining an Object to be examined for Insight; and

- Learning new skills for in-depth interior listening.

Objects for Insight
In our structured meditation, we usually decide in advance to focus our attention on a particular "Object" to be explored. (Alternately, particularly in Zen Buddhism meditation, we can "clear the mind" and let the object arise on its own during the meditation practice.) By "Object," we refer to any concept – material or immaterial, sentient or non-sentient, human or non-human, etc. – that we wish to explore and into which we seek to enhance our Insight.

In the classical Buddhist Vipassana (Insight) meditation practice of southeast Asia, three fundamental Buddhist concepts are contemplated: impermanence (all things change); no-self (nothing exists independently); suffering (what things are versus what we wish them to be). Any one of these concepts can be applied to contemplations about a specific topic that falls within four categories of Objects: the body (and the individual parts thereof); our sensations/feelings; our mind/consciousness (our thoughts and beliefs); selected Buddhist teachings (the Dharma).

Alternative Objects for Insight to these Vipassana objects can be literally anything that exists externally in the Universe and our human experience: the physical world, the metaphysical universe, a philosophical construct, beliefs, ideas, social structures, human conduct, relationships, etc.

Suppose we choose to pursue Insight on "External Objects" (i.e. our surroundings); for example, why *other* things think or act the way they do. For this kind of pursuit, we need to develop the skill to see external objects, or life patterns and structures, as if we were a first-time visitor to Earth observing our civilization and our form of Life, with minimal-to-no preconceptions and assumptions about that Object. In this mental setting, what we encounter is seen as brand new to us, inexplicable on its face, which therefore requires us to examine it closely with an open mind, and draw conclusions only as warranted.

Another approach to identifying an Object worthy of our investigation is pursuing Insight on "Internal Objects" (i.e. our Self). For example, why we think and act the way we do, or what it is that we believe. For this kind of pursuit, we will need to develop the skill to see our Self as if we were standing on the outside looking in at our Self, rather than from our normal posture of seeing from the inside and projecting out. We will need to be able to see our "Self" as separate from our usual sense of Self for the duration of our meditation, positioning ourselves as a second-party outsider watching what we are doing and listening to what we say. It is as when we watch a movie where the character is engaged in action, but speaks to us in voice-over, commenting on what s/he is observing and thinking about the action on display.

Becoming a Deep Listener

People engage in conversation every day, and depending upon their daily roles, may spend an inordinate amount of time in conversation. Business conversations, planning conversations, teaching conversations, social conversations. You would think that, by now, we would be pretty good at it. But many of us are not. Most of the time we are focused on talking at one another, not on really listening to what is being said to us. Talking and listening both require good skills, yet _listening is a significantly different skill set than talking_. Usually we are unaware of that difference because we assume that they automatically go together. They do not. They each function on their own, and some of us are likely better at one than the other.

Using meditation for Insight is a "listening" experience, not a talking one. It borrows from, and builds upon, the skills we need as a listener in everyday life, skills that we normally do not think of developing. Insight Listening is the result of a "teacher/student" dialog with your inner Self. It is a one-sided conversation in the style of the Buddha/student format dialog, or the question/answer "Socratic method" method of teaching.

In thinking, the conscious mind – our ego self, our everyday mind, the "person" we typically think we are – is the Speaker, talking to us non-stop and leading the discussion. In an Insight conversation, the conscious mind is the Listener, not the speaker. The conscious mind serves as the Interviewer, and the willing Listener to what is said. The conscious mind asks questions; it makes no declarative statements. It tells none of the stories we so love to tell about ourselves and our life. It does not speculate about answers. It does not offer opinions. It does not make judgments. It does not draw conclusions. The sole purpose of the conscious mind is to continually Ask the next question that arises from the previous answer, and then Listen to the next answer that returns.

Instead of the usual conscious mind, the Insight thoughts within become the Speaker. It is that little voice that resides within each of us that transcends the mind/ego. By whatever name you may refer to it (Soul; True Self; Higher Power; Imagination; Intuition; etc.), it is there, it is real, and it periodically works its way into our consciousness by its own will. It speaks to us when we open ourselves to it. In Insight Listening, this is voice we are looking to hear, the voice that rarely pierces through the noise of the conscious mind, the voice that needs to be convinced that we are ready to hear what it has to say.

In this Insight conversation, our conscious mind (the Interviewer / Listener) poses an initial question regarding the identified Object. We then sit quietly, awaiting and listening for whatever response arises. Whatever we may "hear" back, all thoughts and responses are acceptable *in the moment.* No value judgements about our Self

46

are made; no conclusions are drawn. We just listen and hear. The next appropriate follow-up question to the response is then asked. This dialog is repeated over and over: ask the Question; wait and Listen for the Answer.

"Let go of your mind and then be mindful.
Close your ears and listen!"
— Jalaluddin Rumi, Sufi mystic

Listening Meditation for Insight – a Process
When we pursue Insight in a meditation setting, we can use a particular form, a step-by-step process to lead us into and through the listening conversation.

1. We continually open ourselves to receiving Insight outside of and during the meditation.
   (Chapter IV, "8 Attitudes for Opening to Insight")

2. We strip away all of our personal attachments, labels, adornments, illusions, prior teachings, and beliefs in order to see what remains ("a blank slate").

3. We put ourselves into a calm, meditative state using some form of Calming Meditation of our choice.

4. We identify an "Object" for our desired Insight (see the ideas above regarding Insight Objects).

5. We clear the mind of our everyday thoughts by letting go of our personal stories, giving up our usual "thinking" in the mind, and focusing our concentration.

6. We "interrogate" the Object and let our internal Insight answer us. We begin this dialog within our mind by asking some short, appropriate starting question about that Object.

The specific question we choose is not critical; anything that can get a discussion going is fine.

7.   We listen *patiently* for what comes back to us. Just wait and listen.

8.   From that first "answer," we start a series of interrogative questions, one at a time, each reflecting the answer we heard to its previous question.
    Examples of Questions: *Why? Why* is that so? *Why* do I think that? *Why* did I do that? Is this *True*? Says *Who*? *Who* did that? *When*? *What* happened? *What* could be a different interpretation?

9.   We continue this process as long as it is warranted and seems productive. At some point, we will just know we are done for this meditation sitting. A quiet peace and completeness typically arises. Or we may choose to cut it short if we feel overcome by our Insights or need to break away for the time being. We know that there is more to know, but we also know we can always return later to pursue this topic further if we so choose. The train of thought, the Insight, will always be there waiting for us.

10. We take a moment to sit quietly, collect ourselves, and express gratitude for the Insight received.

Follow-up to Our Meditation

After our meditation is completed, we go about our normal business and give our new Insights time to settle into our being. In the short-term, we generally avoid thinking too much about these Insights and their meanings so as not to rush to premature conclusions. We let their implications for us evolve gradually.

Sometime after the meditation is completed, we review the dialog that we had. We assess our *structural* handling of our listening dialog. Did we ask effective questions? Did we listen well and manage our responses appropriately? What ideas or modifications do we need to apply to future such meditations?

Subsequently, we assess the *content* aspect of our listening dialog. What did we learn from this meditation dialog? How has this previous lack of Insight affected our thinking, decisions or actions in the past? What will we do with this new Insight in our future? What additional Objects to pursue does this meditation open for us?

Some Additional Suggestions for Being a Deep Listener

Deep Listening is another one of the various skills that we need to develop within the Awareness-Insight-Mindfulness Triad. It is a skill that is beneficial and applicable not only to our internal pursuit of Insight, but also in our daily interactions with others. We need to be as good a listener to ourselves as we would wish others to be with us.

- We should ask good, penetrating questions that are independent of our own beliefs, ones that do not presume a particular or predetermined answer.

- Our interview goal is to follow the trail of questions and responses wherever they may lead us. We must thusly avoid censuring ourselves or editorializing the dialog as it is occurring. Our thoughts and ideas are within us whether we choose to voice them or not. In the end, we choose voicing them to be the positive step for us.

- It is very important to be *patient* between asking the question and the time of receiving a response. A response is typically slow in coming, so we need to let the response arise on its own. Responses that come too quickly are often false ones, coming not from our inner Self but from our ego mind (thinking) trying to assert itself and retake charge.

49

This becomes more especially true the further into the conversation we go. One suggestion is to try to leave at least two breaths between each question, answer, and the next question.

- During the "dead time" between question and response, we can focus on our breath to keep it from wandering into thinking or story-telling mode. Throughout the dialog, we seek to stay quiet and relaxed in the mind.

- We should avoid the tendency to jump to, and be distracted by, what any piece of Insight "means" as it occurs. That interpreting and assimilation process comes later.

- As a Listener, it is all about asking the questions that keep the Speaker speaking. It is not about us and our story. It is all about the Speaker, and letting that Speaker be heard.

Deep Listening presumes that nothing is already known. We are starting this conversation from an entirely fresh place. Each individual response we receive is welcome, illuminates some piece of Insight, and simultaneously serves as a springboard to the next Question/Response.

Some Final Considerations Regarding the Pursuit of Insight

Some Insights come very easily, particularly those that come in the early portion of the dialog, and are usually seen by us as very welcome. But some other Insights come very hard, and require going through very scary and difficult truths. Truths that we have avoided, or kept secret, or chosen to ignore as we remain blindly comfortable within our ignorance. Therefore the pursuit of Insight often requires great courage, trust, and support, because we are going up against the powerful force of Truth. But we created our thoughts; with effort, we can always change them. That is what gets us through the barriers, knowing that they are only "thoughts," not substance. Thoughts may scare us, but they cannot truly hurt us.

We will always survive our scary thoughts. If we could not, they would not be revealed to us. That is one of the prime functions of our ego mind – to protect us from our most difficult thoughts. That prime mission – our mental protection – is also therefore one of the most difficult barriers preventing us from achieving Insight. Faced with an undesirable or a perceived "unacceptable" thought, that ego function rises to a full defense of the delicate balance that we have constructed in our mind. That is why reality is often difficult to see and accept. Yet the pull of Insight to see reality anew, clearly and unadorned, in all its both beauty and harshness, has its own strength. It is a strength that can ultimately overcome the resistance of our protecting ego. Once reality is seen, it is irreversible. There is no going back from the new place in which we now find ourselves. A place now informed, filled with the gift of Insight.

> *The further we go in our pursuit of Insight,*
>
> *the more it requires brutal*
>
> *honesty, courage, and openness*
>
> *in order to see a new truth.*

IX. A MEDITATION PROCESS FOR INSIGHT:

PRACTICE EXERCISES

"Sometimes you need to sit lonely
on the floor in a quiet room in order to
hear your own voice and not let it
drown in the noise of others."
— Charlotte Eriksson, songwriter/author

1. Develop your interview and listening skills during your everyday conversations. Practice doing "interviewing" and "listening" at work, or with family and friends. Bring your developing Awareness and Insight skills to bear by a) noticing what is truly occurring during these conversations among all participants, and b) interviewing a conversational partner about a topic s/he clearly has great interest in and would like to talk about in depth. Set a goal to know more factually about that topic of discussion, and to be able to accurately read back how your partner feels about it.

2. As you develop your interviewing experience with others as well as in your Meditation for Insight, make a list of "good interview questions" that helps you to pursue "the interview."

3. Starting with a blank page, write down bulleted observations regarding everything you can think of that describes the characteristics, nature, existence, and life-cycle of a Tree. If

you have not filled at least one full page, you have not thought about it enough.

4. Read the following example of an Insight dialog. Read alone, or share the roles with a friend. Read each sentence of the dialog very slowly; put at least one extended breath in-between each speaker.

"I Went Shopping."

Speaker: "I bought a new pair of shoes."
   Consciousness: Why?
Speaker: "Because I wanted them."
   Consciousness: Why? Did you need them for something?
Speaker: "No, I just wanted to have them."
   Consciousness: Why? Has not having them prevented you from doing something you wanted to do?
Speaker: "No. But everyone's wearing this style, and I don't have a pair."
   Consciousness: Why? Did you buy them just because everyone else has them?
Speaker: "Yes, it makes me feel good about myself."
   Consciousness: Why do you need to be stylistically correct and fashionable?
Speaker: "Because it makes me feel successful, like I fit in with others."
   Consciousness: Why do you feel you do not fit in well with others, or need to fit in?
Speaker: "Because in school my family couldn't afford to spend much on clothes for us children. So the other girls made fun of me and excluded me."
   Consciousness: Why was that important to you?
Speaker: "Because I wanted to be liked by friends in school."
   Consciousness: Why?
Speaker: "Because I didn't feel liked at home."
   Consciousness: Why?

53

Speaker: "Because I was never good enough to be the ballerina my mother herself never became."

Consciousness: Why were you "not good enough"?

Speaker: "Because I hated it, hated all of the practicing, hated being unable to just go out and play with the other kids."

Consciousness: Why did you want to play with the other kids?

Speaker: "Because I was so lonely."

Consciousness: Why did you hate becoming a ballerina?

Speaker: "Because my mother was making me be something besides who I really was, something besides what I wanted to be."

Consciousness: Why did you think you were different than who your mother wanted you to be?

Speaker: "Because I had other talents, other interests, other goals. I wanted to live my life, not hers."

Consciousness: And what are you doing now?

Speaker: "I work as the Director of a nonprofit performing organization, and I hate my job."

The new shoes make us feel better about ourselves, our life. They are a little salve to a nagging pain inside that will not go away. And even if we never actually wear those new shoes, just seeing them sitting in the closet reaffirms to us who we really are deep down. They are a little medallion reminding us of our life-we-wish-we-had, a fantasy that still lives quietly in our mind. A fantasy now covered over in disappointment. All of that from a pair of new shoes, sitting on a shelf at the bottom of our closet.

This is the Power of "Why?" This is the power of a "conversation with myself." This is the Insight from our Meditation.

(Excerpted from "Unlocking the Boxes of Our Attachments," by Randy Bell)

X. MINDFULNESS IS A VERB

"Mindfulness is simply being aware of what is happening
right now without wishing it were different;
enjoying the pleasant without holding on
when it changes (which it will);
being with the unpleasant without fearing it will
always be this way (which it won't)."
— James Baraz, meditation teacher

Today, people often use the word "Mindfulness" in a variety of contexts and with different intentions. It is similar to the classic case of blindfolding a group of people and asking each of them to describe what an elephant looks like by touching it. Depending upon what part of the elephant they touch, and what their life experience and exposure has been, each will derive a different answer – each true unto itself, but incomplete.

With respect to Mindfulness, it may be described as a "state of being," a way of existing in, and interacting with, the world around us. Or it may be described as having a calm, untroubled mind. Within that calm mind, it may be having a clear, laser-like focus as we go about our daily tasks at hand. Lastly, in common parlance today, it may describe "living in the present moment." That is, not letting ourselves be too preoccupied with our past and being stuck in memories of that which has long gone. Conversely, not being too preoccupied with our future, always thinking about what is coming next and moving on to "our next big thing." Living too much in our past or our future leaves little time left in which to be fully engaged and enjoying the life we are participating in right now. Little time left to learn the life lessons that are right in front of us to be learned. Little time left on which to reflect and savor all the many experiences that are happening to us right now.

Each of these ideas and descriptions may provide us with some aspects of what Mindfulness is. That is why we work on these characteristics in our meditation practice – developing a calm mind, strengthening our focus, concentrating on the breath that is happening *in this very moment* to help keep us living in this moment. These aspects provide a foundation and framework for Mindfulness, but do not complete the idea of Mindfulness.

Mindfulness is the *action step* within the Awareness / Insight / Mindfulness Triad. It is not a passive state of existence. Mindfulness is the intentional *result* of Awareness and Insight. Our attention has been engaged (Awareness). From that Awareness, our knowledge has been informed (Insight). Informed and guided by these Awareness and Insight states, we therefore think, speak and act based upon *deliberate intentions, informed understandings,* and *clear decisions appropriate to this moment and circumstance* (Mindfulness).

Mindfulness is acting independently from past rote, unconscious habits in our thinking and responses that we have developed over time. Having cut the binding cords of old habits and thinking, we speak and act not from our unconscious mental reflexes but from a new sense of ease and openness. We are fully engaged in what we are doing right now, with a concentrated focus developed from our meditation practice; we are not distracted by other thoughts that cause us to be only partially paying attention. We are reacting to situations from a full knowledge of our own Self, not playing a false role that others have put upon us or we have put upon ourselves. We are not expecting others to become what we want them to be for our selfish sake; we do not delude ourselves that we are only thinking of "their best interest" if in fact we are not. We are consistently making decisions from the in-depth understanding and broad perspective that our Insight has given to us, working

56

towards the best possible interest and greater welfare for *all* beings as a result of our actions.

12 Examples of Acting Mindfully

- *We are fully engaged with what is happening now, and are not distracted.*

  We pay concentrated attention to what is transpiring. We choose to be emotionally engaged with, but not subjugated or dependent upon, the person or thing with which we are involved.

  From Insight, we use with others the deep listening skills that we have developed. In Mindfulness, our minds and our attention are in the same place.

- *We make genuine decisions about how to think or respond, rather than simply reacting on automatic pilot or reflex thinking born of old, unresolved experiences.*

  As events are transpiring, we pause and *decide* what we will do next. We do not get unduly caught up in the energy and emotions of the moment, and surrender our Self to the actions and dictates of others. We consider the potential consequences of our next thought or action: will it cause injury to myself or to others? Will it bring joy and benefit to myself or others?

  From Insight, we see clearly our automatic patterns, the mental reflexes that too often drive us. In Mindfulness, we choose the life we live, and decide the actions we will take, with a full understanding of our true Self.

- *Being secure in our own Self, we do not feel the need to unnecessarily defend who we are or what we believe.*

We are willing, even often desirous, to hear and consider the opinions of others. When warranted, we are comfortable changing that which we believed before. Yet we feel no obligation to adopt those differing opinions. Nor do we feel an obligation to force our beliefs upon others.

From Insight, we learn our own Truths, and are comfortable in this moment within those beliefs (while always leaving ourselves open to new Insights). In Mindfulness, it is not about winning an argument. It is about continually searching for Truth wherever that takes us, and considering ideas from wherever they come to us. We give up the ideas that no longer stand up; we refine our viewpoints to reflect new knowledge we have gained.

- *We do not base our actions upon old drivers, memories, other people's beliefs, or what others taught us to believe.*
  We live only our own life. We do not live the life of others, or the life others would choose for us. Our decisions are not based upon what others may have told us over the years what were their truths were, however well-intended by them and however deeply we had implanted them in our minds.

  From Insight, we separate out what we have been taught, versus what we have truly learned for ourselves. In Mindfulness, what we believe is based upon our own personal questioning and reflection, ideas proven out by our own broad experience – experience borne out not by our old, likely distorted memories of events formed in the moment, but by the more reasoned thinking of our mature minds.

- *We do not manipulate others or events in order to achieve what we desire for our own benefit and outcomes.*
  We usually have genuinely good feelings for others, and wish the best for them. But too often our judgment is

clouded by having a personal stake in what happens to them, or feel that what they do somehow reflects upon us. Consciously or unconsciously, we insert a piece of our own well-being into our prescriptions for their well-being.

From Insight, we see how our desires have often dominated our relationships with others. In Mindfulness, we are aware of such potential danger, recognize it when it begins to occur, and filter it out of our interactions. Our actions are free from duplicity or selfish motives, but work in the truly best interest of all, giving others the acceptance and freedom to be as they are.

- *We do not use external things to define who we are.*
  We know that our true Self lives inside of us, even as it projects itself outward and we work each day within an external environment. There are many items in that external environment that are necessary to sustain and develop our human form – e.g. water, air, food, and shelter. After our basic necessities are met, everything else we receive is a bonus. A bonus that can give us pleasure and joy, or ease the efforts of our labors, or expand our human experiences. But these bonus items do not define who we are, who that inner Self is. They are not required to fulfill our human existence. They are merely the tools we employ to accomplish our earthly purpose. They are the means to an end, not the end itself, and there is some form of a greater hidden "cost" for having each of them. There is a reason that many of our greatest spiritual teachers lived lives of simplicity, undistracted by a false pursuit, or the weight, of "success" or riches.

From Insight, we understand why *things* – our "toys" – have been important to us to mask our real fears and insecurities. In Mindfulness, we do not give importance to these false pursuits. We always remember to distinguish

59

between what is required, versus what is simply "nice to have" if and when Life should bring it to our doorstep.

- *We do not take ourselves too seriously, nor do we believe ourselves to be too important.*

    Our life is important. We have a job to do within the unknown time allowance made available to us for our Life. But our Life is not the center of everything. We are only part of a larger Whole. And that Whole will still be here long after we have gone away – changed slightly due to our presence, but only ever so slightly. There are currently approximately seven billion people on this earthly planet. In some way or another we will likely *directly* affect thousands of people over the course of our lifetime. (In our spiritual interconnection to all things, all people will be *indirectly* affected by our existence).

    From Insight, we see this Life we are living more clearly, and better understand our place within the Universe. In Mindfulness, we keep a healthy sense of perspective about ourselves. We are able to admit to, and laugh at, our own silliness; wind ourselves back down when we are getting emotionally overly-caught up in our Life; and recognize when our sense of self-importance is moving out of proportion to our truly limited importance. Remembering that humility is a common characteristic among all significant spiritual teachers, we are always on alert to keep ourselves in check and in balance.

- *We refuse to take on the intentions or actions of others.*

    In humility, we accept that we have all we can do to hold our own life together. That is a fulltime job in itself. Yet, left unguarded, we can be easily influenced by someone else's life, and find ourselves taking on and being driven by the emotions, thinking and actions of others.

From Insight, we see how we have gotten caught up in the drama of others and succumbed to their stories. In Mindfulness, we "leave them to them." We do not take on the "stuff" of others. We seek to be helpful to others, but we do not take on other people's problems and life stories for ourselves. There is a line we do not cross, not because we do not care about them, but because we know we cannot live other people's lives for them. In the end, we must get on with living the life only we can live. And that takes most all of the effort and energy that we have to give.

- *We take full responsibility for our actions and speech, and do not blame our conduct, or the end results, on others.*

    It is a natural human reaction to perceive the difficulties that occur in our lives as being caused by others. Occasionally, that is true. But far more often than we choose to admit, we are our own worst enemy. We continually (consciously or unconsciously) put ourselves in bad or impossible situations. We find ourselves once again in situations that we repeat over and over again, even if on the surface they are in disguised forms (e.g. different people involved, yet same story pattern followed). Situations that, in retrospect, we might likely have seen no good outcomes potentially arising. When we have a fallout with another, or exchange a hot-tempered confrontation, we believe in the moment that it was certainly s/he who provoked the disagreement, who escalated the emotions. We are convinced that we were simply the innocent, aggrieved party.

    From Insight, we see how easily old experiences and distorted thought processes can trigger our unhealthy responses to others. In Mindfulness, we accept that we have our own "hot buttons" that can go off in a tense moment. Buttons formed from past experiences and set as hair-triggers deep within our mind, disguised as safety mechanisms to protect us from injury by others. In any

61

confrontation, it is rarely just about "them"; there is always some element about "us." In Mindfulness, we see those hot buttons always on the ever-ready, and we refuse to allow them to be pushed. Or, if already pushed, we hit the "Cancel" button as quickly as possible to defuse those triggers and deescalate the situation before greater damage is done. In Mindfulness, we admit to our portion of culpability to the event, and apologize to all concerned – including ourselves.

- *We do not respond to difficult events from a perspective of "Why did that bad person do that to me?"*

    We are all victims at one time or another. Unfortunately, at times some individual or group will do genuinely hurtful things to us. They can be things that cause us mental or physical harm, from a lesser to perhaps an unspeakable degree. We have a right – albeit a temporary one – to feel and express the pain, humiliation, or whatever range, and in whatever degree, of emotions those times create within us. But then we have to act, to choose what directions we will follow next. We can choose to remain in the painful stage, continually replaying these circumstances in our mind over and over again, and thereby put our life on hold. Or we can choose to leave this event in the past and move on to the future that awaits us.

    From Insight, we see that our reactions to external stimuli are clues to our deeper feelings and thought patterns. In Mindfulness, we accept that we will never fully know what may have motivated another's actions towards us. (Surprisingly, in many instances their motivation may have been quite unaware of, if not benign to, the difficulty it caused for us.) Instead, we cut the binding cords of our hurts and find a way to forgive our perpetrators. We focus on answering the questions more pertinent to our Self from examining, "Why am I angry with that person? Why did I choose to react to this situation the way I did? What do my

62

reactions and interpretations of the event tell me about my Self? What is the alternative state of being in which I wish to live?" It is when we quit pointing fingers outside, and examine what is happening within us inside, that we find the most valuable spiritual learning. Given our inadequacy to fully understand another person's life, we put our focus on the one thing we can perhaps most influence – our Self.

- *We eliminate thinking and speaking about "They" in favor of "We."*

    We are all part of a greater whole, a vast web of interconnections. As suggested above, we are only a small speck on the vast canvass of the Universe. We directly encounter and affect only a small portion of the planet, which gives us humility. Yet we are indirectly tied to all of Creation, a necessary link in the chain that binds us all together. Interconnected with all things, by our actions we each shape others, just as their actions help to shape us. We rarely know the full extent of the casual action we take, the seemingly chance encounter that comes our way, the dominos that fall unseen. Our eye sees only what is immediately around us; our hearts feel the resultant ripples that disappear into the far horizon.

    From Insight, we better understand our Self, and in so doing, are able to make space for considering the worth and needs of others. In Mindfulness, we know that events are always occurring across humanity and Creation, and that we have an unknown but certain impact upon these events. Every link in this chain of connectedness is important in strengthening or weakening the bond. So we make our decisions with consideration for others, even if they are unseen by us. Our sharp, ill-advised words are passed on from person to person, even if it is not our voice speaking. Our thoughtful, benevolent action is likewise felt not only by its intended recipient, but by those that that recipient similarly touches. All our words and deeds are subject to

63

this multiplier effect, and so we continually act in full Mindfulness of our responsibility to the Life that surrounds us.

- *We see with a 360° vision.*
    The Universe is unending. The objects in Creation are uncountable. All of the people alive throughout our human existence cannot be met in one lifetime. Full and complete knowledge is unknowable. All space is filled with both emptiness and matter. Time has been unending and always continues. Today's story is written from yesterday's chapters which will in turn write tomorrow's. Every thing is made up of parts; each part together completes a whole. A flower can be broken down into many component parts and patterns in its cycle of existence. Simultaneously, the parts all merge and disappear into "just a flower."

    From Insight, our mental vision expands enormously as we see things on many different levels. In Mindfulness, we see the detailed parts, while at the same time we also see the combined whole that the parts create. We continually see, and account for, the larger truths and comprehensive context of all things in all that we do. We think out of our "big mind" that sees comprehensively; we act out of our "small mind" that effects the specific. Both serve us well when they work in harmony together, nurturing each other.

Acting out of a state of Mindfulness brings us into true harmony with Life and Nature. But we do not, we can not, simply drop into Mindfulness by our good intention. Just saying we should be and act in Mindfulness is not sufficient. We must do the preparatory work. As we have continually said, it all begins with Awareness. Getting our attention by seeing something *new* that has been in front of us all along. Without Awareness, there can be no Insight. With Insight, we understand the causation and *deeper* meaning of what we see, as well as its *wider* context – a two-directional view.

From that foundation, and only from that foundation, we are then able to act in Mindfulness. Being continually *alert* so as to recognize a situation being presented to us, and then *acting* on it drawing from, and informed by, our full Awareness and Insight.

Awareness **feeds** *Insight* **which feeds** *Mindfulness*. It is a cycle that is constantly repeating. We work diligently on these three separate skills until they seemingly merge together into one *connected, flowing instance* that happens together almost instantaneously. It is a lifetime practice.

> *In Mindfulness we do not react.*
> *We <u>respond</u> to situations by*
> *choosing our best action*
> *based upon our accumulated*
> *Awareness and Insight.*

XI. MINDFULNESS IS A VERB:

PRACTICE EXERCISES

"Respond; don't react.
Listen; don't talk.
Think; don't assume."
— Raji Lukkoor, environmental author

1. Think of individuals who you believe act "mindfully" in their daily life.

   - What general traits about them seem Mindful?

   - In what circumstances have you seen this Mindfulness occur?

   - What aspects would be aspirations for you to learn from them?

2. At the end of a day, assess the occasions where you *practiced* Mindfulness.

   - What was the situation?

   - What was the Awareness you experienced?

   - What were the Insights you had in that moment, or the past Insights you brought into that moment?

   - In what ways did you act in a Mindful manner?

   - Repeat this assessment exercise at least once a week for twelve consecutive weeks.

3. At the end of a day, identify the occasions where you *missed* opportunities to practice Mindfulness.

- What was the situation?

- What caused you to not recognize this opportunity? (e.g. you got get caught up in the heat of the moment; your thoughts were elsewhere than where you were.)

- What "Awareness trigger" could have helped you get started down the Awareness-Insight-Mindfulness path?

- How would you have preferred this event to come out instead?

- Repeat this exercise at least once a week for twelve consecutive weeks.

> *"Acting Mindfully"*
> *is a building-block process of*
> *accumulating Mindful experiences*
> *such that we recognize*
> *repetitive, typical situations*
> *as they are arising,*
> *respond to them in full Awareness,*
> *informed by knowledge gained*
> *from our Insights.*

"Eventually it will become quiet enough so that you can simply watch the heart begin to react, and let go before the mind starts. At some point in the journey it all becomes heart, not mind. ... The mind doesn't even get a chance to start up because you let go at the heart level."
— Michael Singer, spiritual writer

XII. AN A-I-M MEDITATION

In Hatha Yoga, there is a meditation routine called "Salutations to the Sun" that is recommended for practice each morning. It consists of one continuous, flowing motion through a preset series of yoga poses that work together to properly awaken mind and body to the day. Thereby, we awaken to and honor Life itself.

Following a similar idea of a unifying practice to honor the Self, we can do a meditation dedicated to honoring our commitment to the Awareness, Insight, and Mindfulness Triad. We use a meditation practice as our vehicle for this purpose because it is through meditation that we build the strongest skills in living a conscious life.

We begin this practice with a basic Breath meditation.

- We sit erect, but not stiffly, on the floor on our cushion, or in a chair with our feet on the floor. Eyes may be closed, or opened just slightly with a steady gaze in front of us. We put our hands in a deliberate position of our choosing, whether in one of the standard Buddhist or Yoga positions, or a traditional prayer position, or just resting comfortably in our lap.

- We start with three slow, deep breaths through the nose, then settle into a more relaxed breathing cycle. We put our mind's attention on the nose, and feel the breath coming through the nostrils.

- We begin to observe the breath itself, and make mental note of the different characteristics of each breath we take. How the breath feels as it enters the nostrils. The warmth or chill of each breath. The length of time, whether short or long, that the inhale takes. How deeply the breath goes into our lungs.

- We send our breath out into our body. We focus on each part of our body one at a time. We consciously direct the healing gift of fresh air to reach every corner of this our body. It is all done with deliberate intention, in a slow calm motion.

- We collect the old air that has been sitting in our body, and bring it back up to the nostrils. We make a slow, deliberate exhale, releasing the old air. As we noticed the unique characteristics of each inhale, we similarly notice the characteristics of each exhale.

- We then repeat the exercise for the next inhale. And so on.

- At some point we may realize that our attention has wandered away from the nostrils and the breath. We are off "thinking" about some event or "to do" task in our daily life. We do not criticize ourselves for this drifting; it is a natural occurrence. We simply gently return our attention to the breath and nostrils and continue on again.

After a certain period of time, we reach a sense of complete Calmness in mind and body. Mind and body feel totally connected and synchronized. We are relaxed, but fully alert. We are now ready to move to the next phase of our meditation.

We begin a Concentration meditation. We bring our mind into total Focus, i.e. the ability to keep the mind on one topic, one idea, one thought. We quiet the mind, restrain it from its usual tendency to wildly jump around incessantly from one idea to the next.

- We maintain our steadiness of breath, our attention on the nostrils, our observation of how each breath enters and flows through us.

- We being to count each breath. We breathe slowly, and let the air fill our body

- With each slow exhale, we silently count. We start with saying "1" as the breath leaves the body. Move to "2" on the next exhale. Then move to "3" on the next exhale. And so on. After we get to "10," we start over again with "1" and repeat the sequence.

- At some point we very likely realize that we have drifted away, that our mind has wandered, that we have lost track of where we were in the counting. That is OK. We simply go back and start all over again with "1."

- We repeat this exercise with subsequent sets of counting to 10.

After a certain period of time, we reach a sense of complete Focus and Concentration in our mind. We are still relaxed, but fully alert. We are now ready to move to the next phase of our meditation.

We then begin an Awareness meditation. We bring the mind into Awareness of what exists and what is occurring both within and around us.

- We begin with Awareness of our body. We start by noticing our feet. Is there any pain there, or tension that is constricting either foot? Are they relaxed, supple, at rest? Do they suggest strength or weakness? Have we taken proper care of them in recent times?

- We unhurriedly move up each leg and assess the calves, the knees, and the thighs. We make a similar assessment as we did with our feet. What is each part of our body trying to say to us?

- We move to the hip, the pelvis, the midsection, the torso, the arms. We listen closely to the internal organs. They try to speak to us constantly, but we rarely pay much real attention to them. What are they saying to us now?

71

- We move to the neck, face, and all the individual parts of the skull. We encounter all of our physical being. Thereby, we have encountered reality in the one reality closest to each of us: our physical body.

After a certain period of time, we reach a new sense of complete Awareness of our body, and thereby a new awareness of our Self. An Awareness of Self that concurrently attunes us to a new Awareness of our surroundings, the supportive environment in which we live. We are now ready to move to the next phase of our meditation.

We next begin an Insight meditation. We look deeply inside at our inner Self, and bring the mind into an enhanced understanding of who we truly are.

- We ask our Self, who is this person sitting here at this very moment?

- We wait patiently for the quiet answer to gradually come forth.

- We continue to repeat the question after each answer responds.

- We sense that our understanding of our Self is broadening with each reply, deepening with each Insight.

- We ask who we *were*, in order to account for periods past within our lifetime, thereby helping us to understand the transitory, impermanent nature of our life. We once were a child, but we no longer are. Is that child our Self?

- We gradually give away those answers that are merely "roles" we have performed, and begin to look closely at what remains: our True, Unchanging Essence.

After a certain period of time, we reach a new understanding of our Self within. We allow ourselves to spend some quiet moments meeting this True Self. We are now ready to move to the next phase of our meditation.

We conclude this practice with a Mindfulness meditation. We draw from our focused Awareness and concentrated Insight, and engage fully with the Universe in which we belong.

- Our eyes are closed.

- Nevertheless, through our senses we "see" all that surrounds us. Sounds, smells, tastes are made known in our mind. We *sense* without our eyes the presence of other beings, other objects, within our sphere of connection.

- We extend the borders of our sphere of connection, expanding our range wider and deeper into the Universe.

- We come to know our Self as we have not known it before. We feel a lack of separation from all things as we have not experienced it before. We allow our Self to dissolve into "being one with all things."

We slowly and intentionally bring ourselves back to this time and place, now with eyes and mind fully open and conscious. We finish this practice with a personal ritual of our own making: the saying of a prayer(s); the stating of an affirmation(s) of our Being; a thanks of appreciation for our Life and all that we have received; a meaningful reading from one who inspires us. We make quiet time to reflect upon and enjoy what we have just experienced. We make a point to carry this feeling, this understanding, with us as we go about our daily business throughout the forthcoming day.

XIII. WISDOM

"Perhaps wisdom is intellect and experience
filtered through the heart,
where justice meets mercy and compassion."
— Joyce Rawlings-Davies, spiritual teacher

Wisdom is God's gift to us, to be able to gradually see, learn, and act as God sees, learns, and acts. Wisdom is God's curse upon us, disallowing us the escape of living lives of undisturbed ignorance and complacency. Wisdom is God's challenge to us, to focus inward to know our true Self. Wisdom is God's gift to us, in order that we may live in quiet peace within, and for the benefit of, all that surrounds us.

Following the sequential path of Awareness / Insight / Mindfulness, repeated on a consistent basis throughout our lives, brings us to the doorway of Wisdom. It is in Wisdom that we most closely approach our godliness, and it is Wisdom that we are here on earth to develop. Wisdom is not about just being "smart." It is a *knowing* derived from a cycle of thoughts, moving to action, generating reflection, interpreting experiences into learning, which thereby generates new thoughts. It is a continuous cycle repeated in every moment.

> "Wisdom gives life to the Spiritual Person. The Wisdom of the Spiritual Person is shared, not held jealously within. This Wisdom is not loud, not pushed out to where it is not welcomed, not overbearing. It is given when asked, a gift given freely and lovingly, selective to be exactly right for

74

only this person in this particular moment. Once given, it is turned loose, left to flower or wither in the recipient's own spiritual soil as appropriate.

In the Spiritual Person, Wisdom is easily recognizable. It speaks from a depth and breadth of experience and understanding; it is not shallow, superficial, cursory or flippant. This Wisdom is consistent, oblivious to current time and fashionable circumstances, yet always thoughtfully growing, never completed. This Wisdom is always mindful of its consequences and impact, spoken fully in this moment but drawn from a lifetime of continual learning. This Wisdom is at the core of the truly Spiritual Person.

The Spiritual Person is potentially each of us. We have only to listen to our Wisdom and let it grow in every moment, intertwined with all of the other [spiritual] Virtues. We let these Virtues grow until they envelop our every thought, our every word, our every action, in every circumstance, inclusive towards all people."

(Selected excerpted from
"The Seven Virtues of a Spiritual Person,"
by Randy Bell)

We live a "conscious" life in full Awareness, informed by Insight. We live an "enlightened" life in Wisdom. In Wisdom, we properly balance and integrate "thinking" (our rational Self) with "feeling" (our intuitive Self).

> *Think deeply.*
> *See broadly.*
> *Act compassionately,*
> *With good will.*
>
> *This is Wisdom.*

Peace be within each of you.

EPILOGUE

"I have a friend who's an artist and has sometimes taken a view which I don't agree with very well. He'll hold up a flower and say 'look how beautiful it is,' and I'll agree. Then he says 'I as an artist can see how beautiful this is but you as a scientist take this all apart and it becomes a dull thing,' and I think that he's kind of nutty.

First of all, the beauty that he sees is available to other people and to me too, I believe. Although I may not be quite as refined aesthetically as he is ... I can appreciate the beauty of a flower. At the same time, I see much more about the flower than he sees. I could imagine the cells in there, the complicated actions inside, which also have a beauty. I mean it's not just beauty at this dimension, at one centimeter; there's also beauty at smaller dimensions, the inner structure, also the processes. The fact that the colors in the flower evolved in order to attract insects to pollinate it is interesting; it means that insects can see the color. It adds a question: does this aesthetic sense also exist in the lower forms? Why is it aesthetic?

All kinds of interesting questions which the science knowledge only adds to the excitement, the mystery and the awe of a flower. It only adds. I don't understand how it subtracts."

— Richard Feynman, physicist

"Let me tell you a little
something about beautiful.
I don't just live in a beautiful world.
I understand it."
— young scientist, *"Madam Secretary,"* 1/8/2017

ABOUT THE AUTHOR

Randy Bell's spiritual path has taken him to many diverse sources, though he is principally a follower of the teachings of Jesus of Nazareth, Buddha, Lao-Tsu, and has been a Zen practitioner for 40 years. He lives in the mountains of western North Carolina where he is the Founder and Director of Spring Creek Spirituality. He has written twelve previous books, writes two blogs on a variety of spiritual and social commentary topics, offers a mountain spiritual sanctuary for individual retreatants, serves as a guest speaker / session leader, and leads spiritual and personal growth workshops and retreat sessions. He is a member of North Carolina Writer's Network, and Spiritual Directors International.

www.RandyBellSpiritualTeacher.blogspot.com

www.SpringCreekSpirituality.com

OTHER PUBLICATIONS BY RANDY BELL

(Published at www.McKeeLearningFoundation.com)

Books:

God and Me: A Statement of Belief
  ISBN-13: 978-0-9710549-5-0

Lessons from the Teacher Jesus
  ISBN-13: 978-0-9710549-2-9

Lessons from the Teacher Buddha
  ISBN-13: 978-0-9710549-7-4

Lessons from the Teacher Muhammad
  ISBN-13: 978-0-9710549-9-8

Lessons from the Teacher Moses
  ISBN-13: 978-0-9710549-8-1

Buddhism: An Introductory Guide
  ISBN-13 978-0-9710549-1-2

Forms of Meditation
  ISBN-13: 978-0-9710549-6-7

Starting a Personal Meditation Practice
  ISBN-13: 978-0-9895428-0-7

Unpacking The Boxes Of Our Attachments
  ISBN-13: 978-0-9895428-1-4

Career Choices For Your Soul
  ISBN-13: 978-0-9710549-4-3

The Myths Of Our Founding Fathers And Their Constitution
    ISBN-13:   978-0-9895428-3-8

Executive's Guidebook for Institutional Change
    ISBN-10:   0-9710549-0-8

Various other spiritual essays and reference documents.

Blog Commentaries:

Thoughts From The Mountain
www.ThoughtsFromTheMountain.blogspot.com
A social commentary from a spiritual and ethical perspective.

Our Spiritual Way
www.OurSpiritualWay.blogspot.com
sharing our spiritual journeys together.

Contact:

Info@McKeeLearningFoundation.com

Info@SpringCreekSpirituality.com